NEW *Spirals* NON-FICTION

Ground Zero

Chris Culshaw

Published in 2003 by:
Nelson Thornes Ltd
Delta Place
27 Bath Road
CHELTENHAM
GL53 7TH
United Kingdom

05   06   07   08   /   10   9   8   7   6   5   4   3

A catalogue record for this book is available from the British Library

ISBN 0 7487 7246 4

Cover illustration by Paul McCaffrey
Page make-up by Tech-Set, Gateshead

Printed in Croatia by Zrinski

Introduction

On 11 September 2001 a group of terrorists hijacked four passenger planes in America. Two of the planes were from Boston, one was from Newark and one was from Washington.

At 8.46 am one of the planes crashed into the North Tower of the World Trade Center in New York City. A second plane hit the South Tower a quarter of an hour later.

At 9.37 am the third hijacked plane crashed into the US military headquarters at the Pentagon in Washington.

At 9.59 am the South Tower of the World Trade Center totally collapsed from the top down, leaving a huge cloud of ash and dust.

At 10.03 am the fourth hijacked plane crashed in a field in the countryside.

Nearly half an hour later, the North Tower of the World Trade Center fell down too.

These attacks killed over 3,400 people. Three thousand died in the World Trade Center alone.

This story is about Richard 'Pitch' Picciotto, a New York fireman. He was in the North Tower when it went down.

At the time this story was written, no one knows for sure who was behind the attacks. But America's FBI suspect a man called Osama bin Laden. He's the leader of a terrorist group called al-Qaeda. There's a $5 million reward for information that will lead to bin Laden's arrest.

1

My name is Richard Picciotto. My friends call me Pitch.
I'm chief at the firehouse on West 100th Street, New York.
This is the story of a day in my life. A day I'll never forget:
Tuesday 11 September 2001.

I was working the nine to six shift. I had to leave home by
6 am to get to the firehouse for 7.30. I live in the town of
Chester, about 140 km from New York.

I said goodbye to my wife Deb and my kids, Steve and
Lisa. I stopped on the way to get some bagels. We
always bring in breakfast for our mates who've worked
all night.

I drove my old blue Honda into the city. I'd driven that
way many times. I knew every pothole and every spot
where the traffic jams up. I got to the firehouse in good
time.

I grabbed a cup of coffee and a bagel and went into my
office. It had been a quiet night. Nothing much had
happened. I had some reports to catch up on and settled
down to work.

At 8.46 am I got a phone call. The voice said, 'Stop what
you're doing and turn on Channel Seven.'

I turned on the TV. Two or three of my men came into my office. We all stared at the screen.

'What's going on, Chief?' one of the men asked.

I could only shake my head. What we saw would change our lives for ever.

2

Smoke and flames were pouring from the World Trade Center. The TV announcer said a plane had crashed into the North Tower. We watched the pictures in silence. We were all thinking the same thing. The World Trade Center was one of the tallest buildings on earth. How were we going to fight a fire in a building like that? We were looking at a firefighter's worst nightmare.

But it was worse than a nightmare. I knew the crash was no accident. I knew it must have been terrorism. There had only been one real accident where a plane hit a New York skyscraper. That was in 1945, in thick fog. In those days, pilots didn't have the safety aids they have today. And nowadays no one is allowed to fly over the city anyway.

That morning was cloudless. Perfect flying weather. It couldn't have been an accident. Somebody had flown into the North Tower on purpose. The North Tower was a terrorist target.

I stared in horror at the TV screen. How do you rescue people trapped in that sort of fire? How do you fight a fire so far above ground?

I pulled myself together and grabbed the phone.

'Central control? This is Chief Picciotto. I was at the World Trade Center in 1993. If you need me, let me know.'

In 1993, terrorists had planted a bomb at the Center. The bomb had killed six people and injured over a thousand. I'd been the second chief on the scene. I knew the building. I knew the stairwells. I knew what it was like trying to get people out of a building like that.

I went to watch the news with the other men. Everyone was crowded around the TV. I could see from the smoke it was a very bad fire. People on the upper floors were in great danger.

A fireman said, 'A lot of people are going to die today.'

'Yes,' said someone else. 'And a lot of firefighters too.'

Nobody spoke. If we were called to the fire, would it be us?

3

The TV pictures showed a hole in the tower where the plane had smashed into it. Above the hole the tower was hidden by thick smoke. Smoke is a bigger killer than fire.

Some of the men grew tense.

'Why are we standing here, Pitch? Let's get down there!'

'He's right, Pitch!'

'Don't wait for central control, Pitch. Let's go now!'

As they spoke, another plane smashed into the South Tower.

We couldn't believe what we were seeing. No one said a word. Our eyes were glued to the TV. It was like a bad dream.

I grabbed the phone.

'Central control, this is Chief Picciotto. A second plane's hit. I'm on my way.'

A single word came down the wire: 'Go!'

It's 130 blocks from the firehouse to the World Trade Center. I had to get there fast. I needed a good driver and I had the best – my assistant, Gary.

The other men wanted to go with us. But they had to wait for the order from central control. They had to go to the fire as a team and work as a team.

'Get ready,' I told them as I left with Gary. 'Wait for the call and wish me luck.'

Gary's a brilliant driver. I'd been with him on hundreds of call-outs, but I'd never seen him drive like this before. The pick-up roared down the street with its lights and sirens blazing. We must have reached 60 miles an hour as we raced through the streets.

While Gary drove, I struggled into my fire-fighting gear. I was being thrown about inside the cab. I couldn't stop thinking of the horrors we'd find when we got there.

I tried to snap out of it.

'Think straight!' I told myself. 'You'll be no good to anyone unless you think straight. What equipment do you need? Who do you report to? How do you get to the fire if the lifts are not working? Or if the stairs are out?'

All this was going through my mind as we raced towards the World Trade Center. 'This is war. And very soon I'll be on the front line.'

The funny thing was, I wasn't thinking about my wife and kids. My mind was fixed on the job and on what I'd do when I got there.

4

We got to 20th Street about eight minutes after leaving the firehouse. The other streets were closed to normal traffic. Gary dodged in and out of fire engines and police trucks. We stopped on West Street. This was as close as we could get.

There were people everywhere. They were like a wave moving north, away from the World Trade Center. They were calm. But I could see fear in their faces.

I grabbed my torch, mask and air tank. I didn't take anything else that could slow me down. Apart from my megaphone. It had come in useful in the 1993 bombing. It might be handy again.

Then something made me look up.

Both the North and South Towers were on fire. The upper floors were hidden in clouds of black smoke. But below, where the planes had hit, it was clear. So were the entrances to both towers. With luck, the stairs would also be clear and some of the lifts might still be working. I could only hope.

I left Gary by the pick-up and made my way to the North Tower. Up above, the fire was using up the oxygen from inside the burning offices. People trapped there were throwing tables and chairs through windows to get air. Glass and furniture were falling all around me.

Then I saw something I'll never forget. I saw people jumping from the burning building. At the time, I didn't feel anything. I was numb. All I could think about was getting into the North Tower.

I said to myself, 'Pitch, people are jumping out of this building and you're rushing to get into it. You must be crazy!'

But my job was to get into the building. To put out the fire. To save lives.

After a heart-stopping dash, I reached the front of the North Tower. The entrance was through a set of turning doors. The police and fire crews didn't have time to use them. They'd smashed their way into the lobby. People were going in and out through a huge hole.

I ran inside. There was an emergency command centre just inside the lobby. I knew the fire chief in charge. His name was Pete Hayden. I could see a lot of firefighters in the lobby, waiting for orders. There must have been ten chiefs trying to talk to Pete. They wanted to get their crews into action there and then.

I knew I should have waited until I had an order from Pete. But I had to get up to the fire floor. I couldn't wait. I crossed the lobby and spoke to a crew from the 110th Brooklyn firehouse.

'Are your men ready to go?' I asked.

'Yes, Chief.'

'Got your tools? Extra cylinders?'

'Yes, Chief.'

'Pete!' I shouted to the fire chief. 'I've got six men ready to go. What do you want me to do?'

'Pitch, I've got office workers trapped on the 21st and 25th floors –'

He didn't need to say any more. I knew what to do. Find those people. Bring them down.

'We're on our way,' I said.

5

It was now 9.45 am – three and a half hours since I'd left my home in Chester.

The North Tower of the World Trade Center had three stairwells – A, B and C. Stairwells A and C were at the corners of the building. Stairwell B was in the middle.

Office workers were pouring out of Stairwell B into the lobby. Most were in shock. Some were having problems breathing. They moved quickly, but there was no panic. No pushing or running. Many were helping each other. They looked worn out.

The stairwells were only wide enough to take two people side by side. If we took the stairs to the 21st floor, we'd have to push our way past thousands of people coming down.

'The stairs will take for ever,' I said to myself. 'There's got to be an easier way.'

In a high-rise fire it makes sense to use the lifts. But only if they're safe. There were 99 lifts in the North Tower. I thought one of them must be clear.

I saw two men getting out of one of the lifts in the lobby. I ran over to them.

'How far up does this thing go?' I asked.

'Floor 16,' was the answer.

I saw another fire chief, John Paolillo. I said I was going to use the lift to get to the 16th floor. He told me this wasn't a good idea. He was taking his men up the stairs.

'John,' I said. 'I've got six men and a load of gear to get up to the 21st floor. The stairs are packed with people. I've got to use the lift.'

By now, I knew that two planes had smashed into the towers. I knew that each plane carried 90,000 litres of fuel. This could have spilt over into any of the lift shafts. There was a big risk of fire. That was a risk we had to take.

I told my team to get into the lift. I pressed the button and the door closed behind us.

'OK,' I said to myself. 'This is it. No going back now.'

There was an eerie silence. Then the lift began to rise.

6

We stopped on the 16th floor. It was like a ghost town. It looked as if all the workers had left seconds ago. Computer screens were still on. The desks were littered with cups of coffee and half-eaten muffins.

I told the men to head for Stairwell C. We started our climb up to the 21st floor. It was about an hour since the first plane had hit. There was still a stream of office workers coming down the stairs. But nothing like the crush I'd seen in the lobby.

The 21st floor was a ghost town too. I made a quick search. I banged on every door and yelled, 'Anyone here?' My voice sounded strangely quiet.

I switched on the megaphone and yelled again. There was no reply. We made our way up to the next floor.

There were already firemen on the 25th floor.

'I was told there are people trapped on this floor,' I said to the officer in charge.

'I was told the same thing,' he answered. 'We searched the whole floor and found no one.'

I got my men together. I had to plan my next move. They were all carrying heavy gear. I could move much faster on my own. I decided to go up by myself.

I put a man in charge of the others and made for the stairs.

'I'm going up to the fire floor,' I told them. 'I'll see you up there. Check each floor as you come.'

I set off up the stairs again, moving fast. I passed other firefighters. They were moving more slowly because they'd carried heavy gear all the way up from the lobby.

When I reached the 35th floor, I saw a group of about 40 firefighters and police officers standing by the lifts. They all looked worn out. I wanted to find out what they knew about the fire. I started to walk over to them.

It was then that I felt the building shake. A noise like thunder echoed through the tower. I was inside an earthquake.

We all froze. I tried to make sense of the noise. I thought the lift cables had snapped and the lifts were plunging down the shafts. I was sure that the roof would cave in at any time and bury us all.

It didn't happen. The noise and the shaking stopped.

I looked around at the others. We had no idea what had caused the noise. We didn't know it then, but we had just heard the South Tower go down. All 110 floors of it.

I came out of a daze and found the other men looking to me. Someone had to take control. Someone had to give the orders. I was the senior officer on that floor. That someone was me.

I had to make a big decision. Do we carry on up the tower or do we go down?

It was now over 70 minutes since the first plane hit. Anyone trapped above the fire would be dead by now.

There was only a small chance of saving a few lives if we went further up. But there were hundreds of rescue workers here on the 35th floor and below it. It was my job to try to get them out of the tower. I made a decision.

I decided to retreat.

7

'It's time to move,' I yelled. 'Drop your tools. Let's get out of here!'

I ran with my megaphone to each of the stairwells.

'This is the fire department. Get out! Leave the building now.'

We checked each floor as we made our way down. Some of the offices had glass walls. They were easy to check. Others were closed. I had to run from one the other, banging on doors. When I knew one floor was clear, I ran down to the next.

The stairs were choked with rescue workers. They were all moving slowly. There was no panic.

On the 27th floor, I looked into an office and saw a man sitting at a computer. He was typing on the keyboard. He must have known what was happening. But he kept banging away at the keys.

'What are you doing?' I shouted. 'I gave an order. Clear the building.'

He didn't take his eyes off the screen. 'I'm doing something very important here.'

I was blazing mad. I was risking my life for this man.
Everyone's life was in danger. Mine. His. The rescue
workers'.

I grabbed him by the shirt and pulled him off his chair. He
looked at me as if it was me that was crazy.

'Get this idiot out of here!' I yelled. Two firemen led him
away.

It was now 10.15 am – an hour and a half after the first plane
struck. As I moved down the stairs, a firemen stopped me.
He asked me if I'd seen his team mate. He had to know if
his mate was safe.

I knew the only way to get him to move was to tell a white
lie. I said, 'Yeah, I saw him. He went down the other
stairwell. He'll be OK. Keep moving.'

I told the same white lie many times that day.

8

We reached the 20th floor. I was thinking, 'We'll be out in no time.'

But when we left the 17th floor we found Stairwell C clogged with rescue workers. I pressed forward as far as I could.

'What's going on?' I yelled through the megaphone. 'What's the hold-up?'

The news from down below was passed up to me. The way down was blocked. When the South Tower collapsed, glass and concrete had been thrown into the stairwell.

I ran back up and raced across to Stairwell A. The problem was the same there. I ran to Stairwell B. It was clear.

'Pass the word downstairs,' I called out. 'Come back up to 17. Use Stairwell B. Tell everyone B is clear.'

We got down to the 12th floor. I ran from office to office banging on doors, shouting, 'Get out! Leave the building!'

I opened one door and saw an office full of people. They were sitting quietly. There was no panic, no fear. They were all very calm.

I called down, 'Clear a path! Office workers coming through. Make way.'

I went back into the office and spoke to the workers. 'Go to Stairwell B. Move as fast as you can. There are firemen on the stairs. They'll help you down.'

As the office workers started to leave, I got the shock of my life. There were people in wheelchairs, people walking with sticks and walking frames. Some were as old as my grandparents. Many looked ill. Some had climbed down 70 flights of stairs.

They were not all old or slow-moving workers. Able-bodied people had stopped to help those having problems getting down. I did a quick count. About 25 people in the office needed help to walk.

I told the able-bodied people to get out of the building. I had 60 trained firemen standing by. They'd help the slow-moving workers down the stairs.

It was easy to move the workers in wheelchairs. The problem was the people on foot. They could walk, but only slowly.

I told these people to sit in chairs. Then teams of firemen started to carry them down to safety.

The last person to leave was Josephine Harris, a 59-year-old grandmother. She was carried down by a team led by Jay Jonas, a friend of mine.

We were not far from the lobby now. We moved slowly and steadily. The minutes ticked by. I wanted to run down the last few floors, but I had to keep myself calm.

It was 10.29 am. I was in the stairwell below the 7th floor when I heard the same terrifying roar I'd heard before. This time I knew what it was. We all knew what it was. Three hundred metres above our head the North Tower was breaking up.

9

My mind went numb.

I thought about my wife and kids. I wasn't scared of dying. But I was scared of pain. To me, that was worse than death.

'Make it quick. Please God, make it quick,' I prayed.

I was on the landing when it hit. Every bone in my body shook. I could hardly stand up. The noise was ear-splitting. There was a howling gale. I felt like I was trapped in a wind tunnel.

The building was breaking up all around me. The floor opened like a trap-door. Everything seemed to be happening in slow motion. I was falling down the stairs, but the stairs were falling with me. Then the lights went out.

I stopped falling. I couldn't see and I couldn't move. It was pitch black. I thought I was dead. Slowly I began to feel my body. I moved my fingers, then my legs. I was covered with a thick layer of choking dust. It was in my mouth, my nose, my eyes.

I sat up. I checked my body. No broken bones. I didn't seem to be bleeding. I was alive. I'd been buried alive under the rubble of 100 floors. Thousands of tonnes of steel and concrete and glass.

'Is anyone here?' I called. It didn't sound like me at all. My voice was choked with dust. I tried again.

'Is anybody here?'

No answer.

My voice had a hollow sound. I was in a void. A void is like a cave under the rubble. I called again.

'Can anyone hear me?'

This time I got an answer. The voice seemed to come from below. 'I'm here.'

Then I heard another voice. It sounded far away, below me in the dark.

'I can hear you.'

Seconds later I heard a third voice. This time it came from above.

'I'm here too. I can hear you.'

Three voices. Then there were more. I wasn't alone.

I couldn't see my own hands. It was as black as coal. I had a small torch on my belt. I tried to reach it, but couldn't. I didn't want to make a sudden movement in case the void collapsed.

Slowly my eyes got used to the darkness. I looked up and saw a light. One of the emergency lights in the stairwell. It gave me hope. I needed to know who else was alive and what gear they had. I called out, 'This is Chief Picciotto. Who else is here?'

One by one the men called out their names. A few seconds later I heard Jay's voice. He'd been lucky. All his men were alive.

It was clear we were all in great danger.

'Don't move,' I told the others, 'This place is like a house of cards. It can come down at any time.'

I saw a light below me. Someone had found a torch. With its help I found mine too. Now I could see where I was. I'd fallen about 20 metres into the void. I was lying on a pile of rubble. Above me I could see a flight of stairs. They ended in mid-air. Above them I could see Jay and his men. And Josephine Harris.

I counted six people below me, eight above me and five or six more nearby. Between us we had axes, hooks and 50 metres of rope.

I shouted up to Jay, 'Can you see any way out up there?'

He said, 'It's hard to see. But I don't think there's a way out.'

I called out to the men below, and got the same answer.

I told everyone to try their radio. No one could get a signal.

'Keep trying,' I said. 'There must be someone out there.'

I tried all six radio channels. It was over an hour before I got an answer.

The voice was very faint.

'Stay on!' I shouted. 'Don't leave us here.'

There was no answer.

'Mayday! Mayday! We've got people trapped here!'

I'd lost him.

10

Another voice came on the radio. I knew it well. It was Mark Ferran, the fire chief from Harlem.

'Mark, it's me, Richard Picciotto. I've got people here. North Tower. Stairwell B.'

'Where?'

'The North Tower.'

The radio went dead.

Mark had a rough idea where we were. He got together a team of eight firefighters and set off to search for us. I didn't know then that there was just a pile of rubble where the towers had stood. I knew nothing of the scene outside.

I found out later that Mark and his team had to climb in and out of wrecked buildings. The air had been thick with soot. They'd had to find a way through the fires. Time after time their way had been blocked. They'd had to go back and start again.

Mark came on the radio again. 'We can't find a way through. Hang on.'

Suddenly I felt very tired. All I wanted to do was lie down. I drifted in and out of sleep.

I opened my eyes and saw a pinprick of light high above me. I realised what it was. A patch of blue sky. The dust and smoke outside were clearing. I could see daylight.

I got on the radio right away. 'Mark,' I said. 'I can see sky.'

'Great,' he said. 'Now we've got something.'

I shouted up to Jay. He was closer to the gap.

'Can you climb up to that hole, Jay?'

'I don't think so. The rubble's unsafe. If it comes down it'll kill everyone in the void.'

I decided to move up to where Jay was perched with Josephine and his men. I climbed over piles of concrete and steel. I moved very carefully. I breathed a sigh of relief when I got to Jay.

The hole was just 15 metres above us.

'That's our way out of here,' I told him.

'How are you going to get to it?' he asked.

'Don't worry,' I said. 'I'll get to it.'

The climb was easier than it looked from below. I pulled myself up the broken stairs. Five minutes later I was crawling out of the rubble. The light was so bright it hurt my eyes. I looked around. There was no sign of life. No movement. No noise. Just the rip of the wind across the waste.

I was looking out of a hole in the side of the stairwell. There were huge clouds of smoke and dust blowing across the rubble.

I got on the radio to Mark.

'Mark,' I shouted. 'I'm out. I'm right here.'

11

I thought Mark would be close enough to see me. He wasn't. Neither was anyone else. I could see nothing but rubble. It was as if the whole of New York City had been smashed to bits under my feet.

By now Jay and the others had climbed up to join me. There were fires burning all around. The buildings nearby looked as if they might go down at any moment.

The megaphone was also a siren. I switched it on and gave three loud blasts. Mark radioed through.

'I can hear your siren. But I can't see you. We can't get to you. Every path's a dead-end.'

I looked over the wreckage. There were no people. No dead or wounded. No noise. No lights. No sirens.

I didn't want to wait for the rescue team any longer. The only thing moving was the smoke in the wind. I wanted to get out of there. We'd come this far on our own. We'd make it the rest of the way too.

I fixed the rope to my belt and started to move down. It was then I saw a yellow fireman's helmet. And it was moving.

I put the megaphone to my lips.

'Over here!' I yelled.

The rescue team were just a few minutes away.

12

My heart sank when I saw the rescue team. They were less than 20 metres below us. But they had no rescue gear with them. How were they going to get to us?

I decided it was safer for us to climb down to them. I used the rope, and the others followed. Josephine Harris couldn't climb down. Jay stayed with her. The rescuers climbed up our rope and took over from him.

It was then that Mark Ferran came on the radio. 'You've got to get out of there, fast.'

There were fires burning out of control all over the wasteland. I looked around. Piles of rubble lay everywhere, but they were not as high on the west side. I told Mark that was the way I was going to go.

Mark could see much more from where he was.

'You can't go west,' he said. 'It's too dangerous.'

We began climbing in and out of the rubble. We came to a jagged beam that had fallen across a heap of twisted metal. It looked like the only way forward. I went first. The beam moved with every step I took, but I made it.

The next man to cross was a big guy. He got half way along the beam and froze.

'I can't do it, Chief.'

'Yes, you can.'

'No, I can't. I'll go back. I'll find another way.'

'There is no other way.'

I wanted him to cross. I wanted the other men to see him do it.

But he wouldn't move.

'I'll bet you a hundred dollars you can do it with your eyes closed.'

He looked at me. He looked at the beam.

'Do it,' I said. 'A hundred bucks.'

'You're crazy!' he said.

'Do it,' I repeated.

He walked across the beam as if it was nothing at all. He said I owed him a hundred dollars.

'No way!' I said. 'You had your eyes open.'

It was impossible to tell which way we were going. There were no markers. Just deep holes in the rubble, like moon craters. When we climbed down into one of these holes we couldn't see anything but twisted steel.

Thick black smoke rose from the rubble. My eyes were burning. I could hardly see. Away from where the towers had stood other buildings were on fire.

Mark came on the radio. Once again he warned us, 'Don't go west!'

It was now three in the afternoon, six hours after the first plane struck. As we picked our way over the waste of Ground Zero, I thought about the thousands of people who'd been killed when the towers went down. We hadn't seen a single body. No clothing. Nothing human.

It was 45 minutes after leaving the stairwell that we met two firefighters. I told them about Josephine Harris and the others we'd left behind. Further on I saw another group of firemen. I told their chief there were still people in the rubble. He told me the fire department wasn't sending anyone in. It was too dangerous.

'You've got to do something!' I shouted.

But there was nothing he could do. He had his orders. He had to do things by the book. I shook my head. I was trying to grasp what was real and what wasn't. I staggered out of Ground Zero and found myself on the pavement.

13

'Pitch, we all thought you were dead!' It was Eddie Mechan, one of my men.

Eddie told me Gary, my assistant, had been injured when the towers went down. A lot of my men had been called to the fire. Some had survived because they ran the right way when the building started to fall. Others had been killed because they ran the wrong way. I was lucky. I could hardly stand up, but I was alive.

I stayed on the radio. What had happened to Josephine Harris and the others in the stairwell? At just after 6 o'clock I heard some great news. They'd been pulled to safety.

I had a terrible pain in both eyes. The dust and smoke had almost blinded me. I went to an emergency medical centre. They washed my eyes out with bottles of water. I was taken to St Vincent's Hospital. There I saw dozens of doctors and nurses lined up, waiting for something to do. They'd been waiting to help survivors. They'd wait a long time. There were just 14 of us in that stairwell. Very few others came out alive.

It was 8 o'clock that night when I finally called my wife, Deb.

'Pitch, is that you?' she said, crying. 'I can't believe it. I can't believe it's you. Are you OK?'

I told her about my eyes.

'Can you come home?' she asked.

'Soon,' I said.

I told her I wanted to go to the firehouse first. I'd lost a lot of good men. I was their chief. There were widows to call, friends to comfort.

'See you soon,' Deb said.

'Yes, soon,' I replied.

The end

This story was inspired by *Last Man Down: The Fireman's Story* by Richard 'Pitch' Picciotto (Orion Books, 2002)

The Spirals Series

Plays

Jan Carew
Computer Killer

Chris Culshaw
Gaffs and Laughs
Radio Riff-Raff

Julia Donaldson
Books and Crooks

Nigel Gray
An Earwig in the Ear

Angela Griffiths
TV Hospital
Wally and Co

Paul Groves
Tell Me Where it Hurts

Julia Pattison
Kicking Up a Stink

Bill Ridgway
Monkey Business

John Townsend
A Bit of a Shambles
Chef's Night Off
Clogging the Works
Cowboys, Jelly and Custard
Gulp and Gasp
Hiccups and Slip-ups
Jumping the Gun
A Lot of Old Codswallop
Murder at Muckleby Manor

David Walke
The Good, the Bad and the Bungle
Package Holiday

Non-fiction

Jim Alderson
Crash in the Jungle

Chris Culshaw
Dive into Danger
Ground Zero

David Orme
Hackers

Jill Ridge
Lifelines

Bill Ridgway
Break Out!
Lost in Alaska
Over the Wall

Julie Taylor
Lucky Dip

John Townsend
Burke and Hare: The Body Snatchers
Kingdom of the Man-eaters
Raiders of the Dome Diamond

Keith West
Back to the Wild

Fiction

Jim Alderson
The Witch Princess

Penny Bates
Tiger of the Lake

Jan Carew
Footprints in the Sand
Voices in the Dark

Susan Duberley
The Ring

John Goodwin
Ghost Train

Angela Griffiths
Diary of a Wild Thing
Stories of Suspense

Anita Jackson
The Actor
The Austin Seven
Bennet Manor
Dreams
The Ear
A Game of Life and Death
No Rent to Pay

Paul Jennings
Eye of Evil
Maggot

Richard Kemble
Grandmother's Secret

Helen Lowerson
The Biz

Margaret Loxton
The Dark Shadow

Bill Ridgway
The Hawkstone
Mr Punch
Spots

John Townsend
Back on the Prowl
A Minute to Kill
Night Beast
Snow Beast
Sweet Dreams